The Little Book of
LUCK

Luck is
Simply a Choice

The Little Book of
LUCK

Luck is
Simply a Choice

Leticia Dominguez

www.ourlittlebooks.com

E-mail: sales@ourlittlebooks.com

Printed in Canada.

I dedicate this book in memory of my parents, Dr. Calvin P. Jones, Phd. & Stella Jones. It was through their love and understanding that I learned to appreciate each precious moment of life and respect nature for the beauty she continually gives us. Enjoy with love.

Contents

Luck

"All of us have bad luck and good luck. The man who persists through the bad luck — who keeps right on going — is the man who is there when the good luck comes — and is ready to receive it."
—Robert Collier

Do some people really have all the luck? Are some just born lucky? It sure can seem that way as you watch your co-worker get the promotion you have been diligently working towards. Or, it appears to be just plain bad luck when you total your car.

Good luck seems to follow some people around, no matter what happens. They get laid off from their job and are soon offered a better position and more money. Some seem to walk around with the Midas touch, while you never seem to have enough luck. Why are they so lucky? Is the universe out to get you? Can you remember the last time good luck knocked at your door? You're not alone; many people feel trapped in bad luck.

If you listen to comments throughout the day, you will think we are all a bunch of really unlucky people. We are unlucky at love, unlucky at work, unlucky at home. We have a habit of giving the responsibility for our lives to luck. Someone else always has good luck while we always have bad luck.

What if you could change your luck by making a simple choice; would you?

In this book we will look at turning *Little Unforeseen Circumstances Keeping* you from moving forward, or bad **LUCK**, into life. By stepping back and taking the emotion out of an experience, we can change the way we perceive it. We will examine the unforeseen gifts of living in the moment. We may have to walk in another's shoes or change our current perspective, yet with daily practice, it can be done. If we keep moving forward with a positive attitude, we can bring good luck into *Living Individual Fantastic Experiences — LIFE.*

Luck is *simply a choice.*

Little Things Can Seem So Big

"Shallow men believe in luck. Strong men believe in cause and effect."
—Ralph Waldo Emerson

Webster defines luck as (a): a force that brings good fortune or adversity or (b): the events or circumstances that operate for or against an individual.

Luck is most often referred to as "bad" luck. Every once in a while we hear about "good" luck, but what others see as good luck, we usually call hard work, or say it had nothing to do with just luck. We tend to take the responsibility of life upon ourselves if something is good and blame luck when something is bad. Here's an example.

You're tired, you've worked all day, and finally you're going home. The seven o'clock meeting this morning started off wrong because you had left the material to distribute on your desk. By the time you went back to your office and then returned to the conference room, you were late for the meeting. During the announcements, you knocked over your coffee and stained your shirt. "What's next?" is the question on your mind. Look at all that bad luck!

At lunch, you try to gather your thoughts. Your morning had been so crazy. "Why do I have all the bad luck?", you ask yourself while half-listening to your friends and co-workers discuss this and that. You finish your lunch and get the check, but now you can't find your wallet. You realize you left it at home. Feeling like an idiot, you must borrow money from a coworker.

It's 5 p.m. Finally time to go home. Your mind is filled with all that's happened today, and you just hope no one asks how your day went. You want to forget about all your bad luck and relax as you get into your car and head home.

Suddenly your cell phone rings, and you take your eyes off the road during rush hour to answer the call. BAM, you hit the side of another vehicle. It seems like nothing but bad luck from start to finish today!

You are not hurt, so you get out of your car to see if the other driver is OK. Thankfully, there was no passenger in the other car and the driver was not hurt. But look at your car — it is totaled, and so is the other vehicle. You wonder how you will come up with the money to pay for this.

Finally, you get home, call your best friend, and start describing the horrible day. Each circumstance and experience looms larger than the last. You have convinced yourself that you have the worst luck in the world, and by gosh, you want to let everyone else know it too.

Now let's go back and take a different look. Let's dissect this BIG BAD LUCK day.

Was being late to the meeting <u>that</u> big a deal? If you are not late all the time, and you are usually prepared, then a few minutes would be excused by your associates. You are not expected to be perfect; all you had to say was, "Excuse me, I had to go back to my desk to retrieve some papers." It really wasn't that bad, was it? The coffee.

Oh, the bad luck of spilling coffee on your shirt. But, shirts can be washed or replaced, so really, come on now, it's not a big deal. Think of one person you know that has not spilled something on themselves at one time or another. And borrowing ten dollars for lunch? It might have been embarrassing in the moment, but that's not big, bad luck.

When you look back, all of the bad luck that you were experiencing was only the circumstances of the moment. Nothing life-shattering or devastating happened. Even the car accident was not life-changing because no one was hurt and there is insurance to cover the damage. It is simply a choice as to how "big" and how "bad" you view each event that happened.

Exercise:

For today, try stopping for a few moments and dissect the events that seem too big. Look at what you have accomplished. You will see that everything is composed of little unforeseen events, and that none of us can predict the future. So why stress over the small stuff?

Unforeseen Gifts

"In the middle of every difficulty lies opportunity."

— Albert Einstein

Are there gifts in a day like the one just described? Can you see the gifts, blessings, miracles of those experiences? Start by looking at the events that preceded the "bad luck" and the events that followed. Hindsight is 20/20, and you can choose to understand how lucky you are.

You were a little late for a meeting, but so what? Eventually you were there, alert and prepared. You could have overslept and missed the meeting. You could have been stuck in traffic, or your car could have broken down on the side of the road. Get the picture? There are many worse scenarios. The fact that you were at the meeting at all was actually a gift.

Spilling coffee on your shirt wasn't that bad, now was it? It may have been embarrassing, yet it was not a tragic event. No one's important papers were ruined, you were not burned, and you even got fresh coffee. What some people would give for a hot cup of coffee or a meeting to attend! With unemployment at its highest in years, many would trade places with you in a heartbeat. Actually you're pretty lucky, don't you think?

Borrowing money for lunch is definitely no reason to decide that your day was nothing but bad luck. You had the money to repay your coworker, while many individuals don't have the money to eat three meals a day. So where's the bad luck?

The car accident could have been worse. No one was hurt; that was a miracle in itself. Automobiles are replaceable, people are not, so how could it be considered bad luck? You could have had no insurance and would have had to come up with thousands of dollars for repairs. You could be one of the many individuals or families who can't afford transportation, or never owned a vehicle. You could be someone who can't drive due to blindness or other disorders. Consider yourself lucky here. You drive, you own a car, you had insurance and no one was hurt. Besides, now you get to pick out a new car! A simple choice. See the bad luck or see life.

Exercise:

For today, stop for twenty minutes in the evening and take a glance back at your daily circumstances. You can write down your thoughts or just take time to make an inventory of the choices you made that day. What lessons have you learned? What experiences do you want to repeat? Or not repeat? Make sure when you look back you look at the positive aspects of a circumstance. Seeing the hidden gifts in each circumstance is *simply a choice*.

Control Your Emotions

"What I think and feel and what I get are always a match. And so, if I want something different than what I've been getting, I have to, somehow, generate different feelings."

—Abraham

Emotions are a powerful energy. If we could take emotion and set it aside, then look at the circumstances around us, the outcome would look vastly different. Our emotions color our viewpoint. If we change the "lighting" on any situation, we can see a lesson learned or a hidden blessing for our next adventure, our next step forward.

Emotions reveal a direct view of our past and our beliefs. When emotion gets involved, it can enhance or block the way we see specific circumstances or events. Fear, for example, can keep us from moving forward. If we take fear out of our life's equation, we may see a challenge, but it does not stop us on our journey. Leaving fear in the equation can point you in the wrong direction.

All of our emotions send messages out to the universe. The universe, in its perfect timing and cycles, is giving us back what we are asking to receive. For example, you may say you want a particular event to happen in your life; however, if your emotions are not in alignment with it, you won't attract it into your reality. So how can we set our emotions to be in alignment with what we want?

In our example above, did you want to be late for your meeting? You had no direct desire to be late, but when you realized you would be late, fear took over. You then convince yourself that the rest of the day will be just as unlucky. Your mind starts the "what if" or fear-based version of the moment. What will everyone think if I'm late? What if the meeting started without me, and now I won't get the promotion I have worked so hard for this year? These are fears based on false beliefs and past experiences.

When fear is sent out through our vibrations, we will attract more fear or bad luck. If negative emotions come to the surface, change them and you will change the outcome. Instead of the "what ifs," you could say to yourself, "So I was late, yet I still made a fantastic presentation and had everyone's attention." Change anxiety to appreciation. Taking control of your emotions is *simply a choice.*

How about spilling the coffee, or not having your wallet with you at lunch? You can choose to see the humor in those events or the bad luck. You can see that no one was hurt, or you can choose to point out your clumsiness and laugh at yourself, or you can play the "poor, pitiful me" role. There is no right or wrong in the emotions you feel, but remember that your emotions definitely affect what you attract into your life.

The auto accident described earlier is a prime example of fear, because the fear of what's next comes flooding into your mind. What about the other person involved? Will they sue? What about your car? Will you be able to get another one quickly? The "what if" of the unknown can create fear that invites bad luck to come over and join you.

If we remove the emotion from these questions, we could see a blessing or gift in the incident. Our "what if" questions would turn into positive statements, such as, "Thankfully no one was hurt. Now I can buy the new car I've been looking at. Thank goodness I have full coverage and my insurance will pay for the damages."

By erasing our initial emotions and replacing them with appreciation and gratitude for the positive, we change our perspective and acknowledge the good of the circumstance. Over time, this will become a habit, and negative thoughts will occur much less frequently.

Exercise:

For today, try stepping back after any event or circumstance and look at the positive. Study each event unemotionally, as if you were talking to someone else. What good would you point out to them? Make the choice to do the same for yourself, without fear or negativity. Do not let Little Unforeseen Circumstances Keep you from moving forward; take charge of your luck.

Keep Moving Forward

*"Luck is what happens when
preparation meets opportunity."*

—Seneca

In the last few chapters, we have discussed how Little Unforeseen Circumstances Keep us from moving forward when bad luck appears to follow us around. We know we can break down events and circumstances into small pieces and that we don't have to sweat the small stuff. We have discussed looking for the hidden gifts. We now realize we can eliminate the emotion and see the real picture. Sometimes moving forward seems to be impossible. It's really simple: choose to take one step at a time.

If you do not want to be late to meetings as in our example, leave five minutes earlier than usual so that you have extra time if you've forgotten something. If you leave early, you take the fear out of being late, even if traffic is slower than usual. You are moving forward, one step at a time.

Accidents do happen. Unforeseen circumstances and events will happen unexpectedly — good old Murphy's Law in action. You must make a simple choice about how you will act. Laughter is a great way to lighten up the room, and release positive energy. Laughter truly is great medicine, and helps improve your outlook on life. Don't be afraid to laugh at yourself; others will, too, so why not choose to be the initiator of the positive?

At some point in time, we will also seem stuck. How we react tells the world what we are made of. If you have no money to pay for lunch, ask to borrow it. Luck is not controlling you, you are controlling it. Again, don't let fear or embarrassment take over your emotions. Take the step to correct your error, admit it, ask for help and move forward. It is *simply a choice*.

If you are in an auto accident, you can beat yourself up for not paying attention, you can blame the other person, or you can blame bad luck. You can rely on emotions or you can simply choose to move forward, with a calm and open mind. Start shopping for a new car, contact the other driver and make sure the repairs were done, decide not to answer your cell phone while you're driving. All of these examples are simple choices with big impacts on your ability to move on.

Moving forward does not mean that you ignore circumstances or events. It simply means that there is nothing that can truly hold you back. We will all experience setbacks in our lives, but if we let them control us, we will see that "bad luck" follows us everywhere we go. If we, on the other hand, choose to move forward making our own choices, we will start Living Individual Fantastic Experiences — or experience LIFE. It really is *simply a choice*.

Exercise:

For today, make your "moving forward" list. Look at your current situations and beliefs, and then list the steps you can take to change and move forward. Dare to do things differently! These steps can be as simple as "I will leave five minutes earlier for work" or "I will stop and look at my circumstances without emotions."

Live in the Moment

"Each misfortune you encounter will carry in it the seed of tomorrow's good luck."
—Og Mandino

We have to learn to live in the moment, which does not mean that we don't honor the past or have a vision for the future; it means not dwelling on past circumstances and not setting expectations for the future. Living in the moment is truly *a simple choice*.

We know we can look at the past without allowing our emotions to take control, which allows us to see the inherent lesson and re-write the circumstance. Why not do the same every moment as life unfolds?

The past is gone, we cannot change events. We can, however, re-write our past, or present, at any time.

Let's look at the accident: we were at fault, so how could this possibly work in our favor? We can begin by studying the situation. In this scenario, I answered my cell phone, I was not paying attention, and my car collided with another car. What if we changed the way we spoke about the situation; could we see it in a more positive light?

Try this:

I was in an auto accident. Thankfully, no one was injured, and both parties had insurance to cover the damages. While waiting for the police report, the other driver and I exchanged business cards. She was the Director of a company where I had tried several times to sell my services. After making sure everything was all right, I asked her if she would like to have coffee or lunch in the future. Because of the relationship I began to form with her, I now have the opportunity to sell myself and my services to her company. If the collision had not happened, I would not have made the contact with her, and I would have missed out on a business opportunity.

By re-writing your past, you are not ignoring what happened; you are simply making the choice to live in the moment, seeing the positive, which allows you to move forward. We all have things in our past that we are not proud of or would like to have changed, so now, in this moment, change them, re-write them. Let yourself know that it is all right to view the past as you want to see it in the current moment.

None of us knows what the future holds for us. We have wants, desires, dreams and visions, yet many of us focus our attention on the expectations of the future. If things don't go exactly as we think they should — and they rarely do — we get disappointed or start counting on luck to get us there. Just as you can re-write your past, you can also write your future.

Living in the moment is simply a choice of believing in yourself exactly where you are now. The past impacts our ability to live in the moment, through experiences and false beliefs that we hold onto. The future too can impair our ability to allow the flow of the moment if we just focus on the expectations of the future. We can believe, appreciate and know that right here, right now, *we* are in control of our lives, not luck. Take charge. There is nothing that you have done or will do that can take the control of Living Individual Fantastic Experiences away from you, unless you choose to let go of being in control of your own life. Be in control and do not give the control of your life to luck.

Exercise:

For today, glance back and re-write the past that does not fit into your picture of reality. Then jot down your dreams of the future. Do this without emotion or attachment to outcomes. This will allow you to take a look at the moment, look at where you came from and the direction you are headed. Then you can live in the moment, knowing that you, and not luck, are responsible for your life.

Individual Perspective, Change the Picture

"Opportunity is missed by most because it is dressed in overalls and looks like work."
—Thomas Edison

When we live in the moment, we have our own perspective of the actual outcome. What we choose to see as good or bad comes from within, based upon our beliefs, our past, and from what society tells us is our future. But we can change our views of circumstances and events if we want. You can choose to change the picture.

As we discussed in the last few chapters it is a simple choice. Our perspective of any outcome is unique and created by us in our minds and our hearts. If we don't like what we see or the luck that we are having, we can change the picture. When we watch television, if we decide we don't like what is on, what do we do? We change the channel. Life allows us to change the channel by simply changing our choices.

From a spill to an accident, changing the channel takes practice. We totaled the car, yet we are getting a brighter, newer model. We changed the channel. We run late, so who determines our time and our time frames? We do so by simply changing the channel. If we lined up ten people and showed them the same picture or story, each will have an opinion, a perspective, and a view of what they just saw. Make the choice to see what you want.

If you feel that bad luck follows you around, change the channel, change the picture. You are the only one who can make the choice to keep your current views. You are the only one who knows if your circumstances are for you or against you. You are the only one who can make the simple choice to change bad luck into life.

Exercise:

For today, as events and circumstances pass by, look at each one and decide if you like what you see in this moment. If not, change the channel and take notes. Begin the shift of responsibility to you instead of to luck, by shining the light of awareness upon these moments. Begin to record in your mind and in your heart the changing of your picture of reality. As Thomas Edison stated above, we miss opportunities simply because we cannot see the picture, we only see the disguise.

Focus on the Positive

"To support mother and father, to cherish wife and child and to have a simple livelihood; this is the good luck."
—Buddha

Circumstances and events will happen moment to moment in your life, and whether you choose to see them or not is up to you. There will be setbacks, births of ideas, deaths of old ideas, and this will flow throughout your existence. There will be times of joy and times of sorrow, times of plenty and times of need. No matter what is on your plate, you have the choice to focus on the positive or the negative.

Focusing on the positive assists you in moving forward. Focusing on the positive sends out the vibrations and energies of what you want to bring into your reality. Some see a glass as half- empty, while others see the glass as half-full. Some are pessimists, while others are optimists, it is a choice that we have made.

One way to stay focused on the positive is to remind yourself that there are always people going through a situation worse than yours. On the other hand, there is always someone, somewhere, in a better circumstance than yours. Focusing on the positive and living in the moment is best done by appreciating where you are and who you are.

By appreciating what you have and who you are, you focus on the positive.

Appreciation can be a silent thank-you, sending out the vibrations of attraction for more. Knowing that you are where you choose to be and being thankful for where that is, is a powerful tool. When we appreciate ourselves and circumstances, focusing on the positive of any moment, we are sending out a message of love and control of our life to those around us. Notice how when you are focused on the positive, others around you lighten up and begin to see the positive in their lives.

Focusing on the positive and seeing the "good luck," not the bad, is an example to others. We learn by example, we follow example, and with a simple choice, you can be the example.

Being positive does not mean that good luck or bad luck won't happen. Focusing on the positive, however, does allow you to take responsibility for controlling your own life. Giving your responsibility over to luck will not allow you to focus on the positive, it will allow luck to control you and your individual experiences.

Exercise:

For today, focus on all the positive aspects of the past. Focus on what is good, not bad. Focus on taking back your responsibility and not giving it away to luck. Focus on the individual fantastic experiences. You may want to write them down or not, yet make mental notes and watch the changes in your daily life and the lives of others around you.

Experience Life

"The day you decide to do it is your lucky day."

—Japanese Proverb

When you let little unforeseen circumstances keep you back, counting on luck to provide you love, joy or anything else, you are not experiencing life. Life consists of a multitude of experiences; life will always change, for life is a constant cycle. When you give your responsibilities for life over to luck, you are allowing both the good luck and the bad luck to take control.

You can blame bad luck when you run late for a meeting. You can blame bad luck when you spill your coffee. You can blame bad luck when you have forgotten something or run out of money. You can blame bad luck when you have a car accident. You can blame bad luck for your life, if that is your choice.

In order to actually experience life to the fullest, you must first take responsibility for your choices . You have to decide if the circumstance or event is what you want to continue to create. Once you have made the decision to take back your responsibility, you can live individual fantastic experiences. You will simply have to choose to be in control.

You can decide in any moment to Live Individual Fantastic Experiences — LIFE or if you will let Little Unforeseen Circumstances Keep you from moving forward — LUCK. In order to fully experience anything, you have to decide what it is you want and take the action of moving forward.

The day you take control, is the day you will change your bad luck into life.

Exercise:

For today, take back your power, accept responsibility and record the changes from luck to life. It is a simple choice, and it is yours. Experience life, and don't let bad luck deprive you of one of the most wonderful aspects of being here on this earth.

Turn Luck into Life

"I've found that luck is quite predictable. If you want more luck, take more chances. Be active, show up more often."
—Brian Tracy

You now have a simple choice. You can turn luck into life. Your choice is simply to let Little Unforeseen Circumstances Keep you from moving forward or you can choose to Live Individual Fantastic Experiences.

When you make the simple choice and begin to break down events that are overwhelming and big into smaller pieces of life you can see that noting is as "big" as it first appears.

When you make the simple choice and look for the gifts in your circumstances, your life will begin to look brighter.

When you make the simple choice and take the emotions out and look with clear vision at a situation, you will realize that your emotions cloud your view.

When you make the simple choice and keep moving forward, your steps begin to glide and soon you will be running.

When you make the simple choice and live in the moment accepting responsibility for your choices and actions, you will begin to see that this moment is really all there is.

When you make the simple choice and change your perspective, you will see that things are not always as they appear at first.

When you make the simple choice and focus on the positive, you will begin to see the positive in others and in your life.

When you make the simple choice and take these steps, you will have begun to stop letting Little Unforeseen Circumstances Keep you from moving forward and you will begin to Live Individual Fantastic Experiences.

Luck or Life

The past is now behind us
The future yet untold
The rhythms of the time
Turn our hearts to stone or gold.
The memories of the moments
The experiences of love and hate
Are only just a portion
Of the reality we create.
The past we cannot change
The future we do not know
It is only in this moment
We choose where we will go.

Author Quotes

Robert Collier

Robert Collier (1885–1950) was one of America's original self help authors with his best seller "The Secret of the Ages". Collier wrote about the practical psychology of abundance, visualization, taking action, and being your best.

Ralph Waldo Emerson

Ralph Waldo Emerson (1803–1882) was an American essayist, philosopher, and poet. His teachings directly influenced the New Thoughts movement of the mid 1800s.

Albert Einstein

Albert Einstein (1879–1955) was best known for his Theory of Relativity. He published over 300 scientific works and over 150 non-scientific works. In 1999, Time Magazine named him the "Person of the Century".

Abraham-Hicks

Ester Hicks is an inspirational speaker and best selling author. She is able to translate thoughts from a group of evolved non-physical teachers called Abraham to help people be self-empowered and connected to their inner being.

Seneca

Lucius Annaeus Seneca (4 BC–65 AD), Born in Spain, was often known simply as Seneca, or Seneca the Younger, became a Roman Stoic philosopher, statesman, and dramatist. Eventually retiring as advisor to emperor Nero.

Og Mandino

Augustine "Og" Mandino (1923-1996) born in Italy was a "sales guru" and the author of *The Greatest Salesman in the World*. His books have sold over 50 million copies and have been translated into over twenty-five different languages.

Thomas Edison

Thomas Edison (1847-1931) American inventor and businessman who developed many devices that greatly influenced life around the world.

Buddha

Buddah (563 BCE-483 BCE) was a spiritual teacher in the northern region of the Indian and the founder of Buddhism. During his upbringing as a Kshatriya by birth, he had military training, and because of Shakyan tradition, in order to marry he was required to pass tests to demonstrate his worthiness as a warrior.

Brian Tracy

Brian Tracy born in Canada in 1944 is a self-help author. His talks and seminar topics include leadership, sales, managerial effectiveness, and business strategy.

Suggested Reading

Law of Attraction, **Jerry & Ester Hicks**

This book will show you the omnipresent *Laws* that govern this Universe and how to make them work to your advantage. The understanding that you'll achieve by reading this book will take all the guess-work out of daily living. You'll finally understand just about everything that's happening in your own life as well as in the lives of those you're interacting with. This book will help you to joyously be, do, or have anything that you desire!

Inspiration: Your Ultimate Calling, **Dr. Wayne W. Dyer**

This book shows the voice in the universe calling each of us to remember our pur-pose—our reason for being here now, in this world of impermanence. The voice whispers, shouts, and sings to us that this experience of being in form, in space and time, knowing life and death, has meaning. The voice is that of inspiration, which is within each and every one of us.

Leadership and Self Deception: Getting Out of the Box, The Arbinger Institute

This book uses the story/parable format while taking a novel psychological approach to leadership. It's not what you do that matters, say the authors, but why you do it.

Conversations With God: An Uncommon Dialogue, Neale Donald Walsch

This book is about Neale Donald Walsch's questions to God. As he was writing, he realized that God was answering them... directly... through Walsch's pen. The result, matter of fact, in-your-face wisdom on how to get by in life while remaining true to yourself and your spirituality.

Success Principals: How To Get From Where You Are To Where You Want To Be, Jack Canfield

This book presents sixty-four success principles and draws on the author's own experience and that of others to illustrate them. Each principal receives a concise, easy-to-digest chapter that challenges readers to risk creating their lives exactly as they want them.

The Four Agreements: A Practical Guide to Personal Freedom, Don Miguel Ruiz

In *The Four Agreements* shamanic teacher and healer Don Miguel Ruiz exposes self-limiting beliefs and presents a simple yet effective code of personal conduct learned from his Toltec ancestors. The four agreements are these: Be impeccable with your word. Don't take anything personally. Don't make assumptions. Always do your best.

Affirmations: How to Expand Your Personal Power and Take Back Control of Your Life, **Stuart Wilde**

This book will help you maintain a grip on positive attitude and a positive frame of mind even if it is a daily struggle for you. These affirmations can come to your rescue like an emotional first aid kit. They are targeted and focused on all the specifics we need help with.

Happy For No Reason: Seven Step to Being Happy From the Inside Out, **Marci Smiroff**

This book offers seven clear, powerful and effective steps you can practice to be happier right now. Marci Smiroff interviews 100 Happy people to illustrate that these folks had to "work & create their own well being."